HEREFORD
Then & Now
Volume Three

by Derek Foxton

HEREFORD
Then . . . .

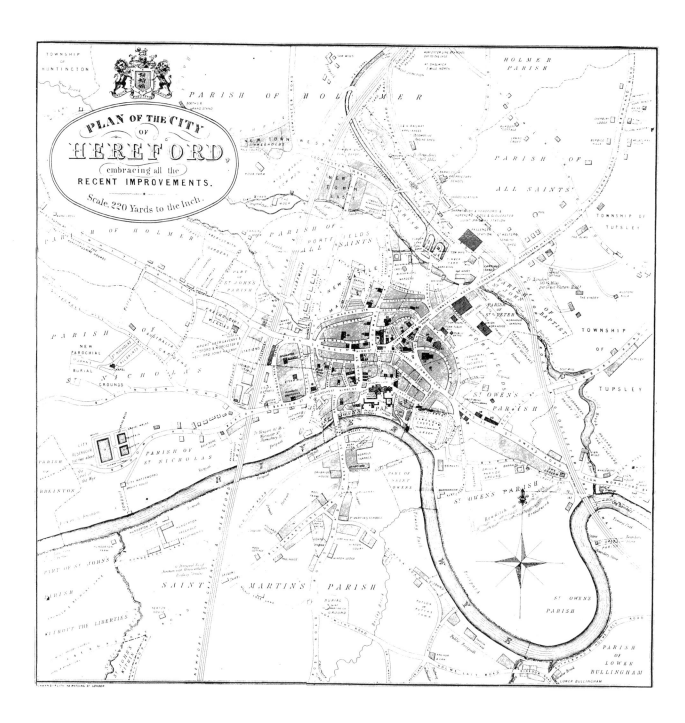

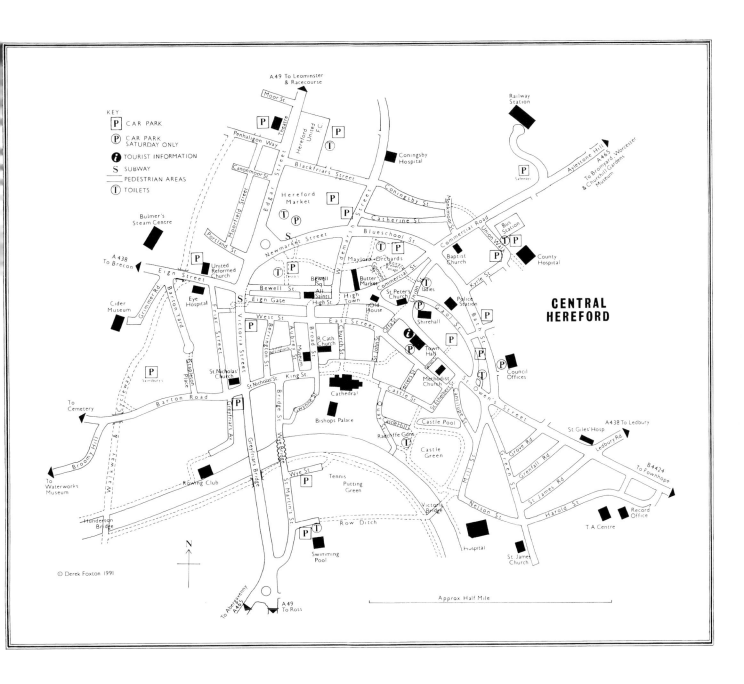

© Derek Foxton 1991

CENTRAL HEREFORD

Approx Half Mile

Published by
Derek Foxton
4 Helensdale Close
Venns Lane, Hereford
HR1 1DP
Telephone: 01432 357315

ISBN 0 9514081 3 5

Designed and produced by
Derek Foxton Publishing

Dust Jacket by
David Postle

Printed by
The Amadeus Press Ltd, Huddersfield

Introduction

It is now nine years since the first volume of *Hereford Then and Now* was published and six years since the second. This third volume contains a selection of previously unpublished old photographs of Hereford and compares them with present day pictures showing the changes that have taken place over the years.

I am very pleased to include two very early photographs of historical importance. The Royal Photographic Society has kindly allowed reproduction of their 1855 Pollock photograph of the Old House and the Old Market Hall which is the only known photograph of the building. The other rare picture, of Broad Street was taken before the Library and City Museum was built.

The photograph of the horse-drawn omnibus in High Town is another gem, reproduced by kind permission of Mrs. Susie Major in memory of her late husband who rescued the collection of negatives taken by the Rev. Skeffington Hume Dodgson, brother of Lewis Carroll, Vicar of Vowchurch 1895 – 1910.

With Peter Deans kind permission I have also used several extracts from the Bustin Collection in the County Records Office, under the supervision of Sue Hubbard.

The lovely print of the Old Wye Bridge with a sailing boat and paddle steamer has been kindly lent to me by Basil Butcher, since when it has been donated to the City Museum. Basil has also been an invaluable adviser on historical accuracy and detail over many years.

In this book I have used extracts from publications by Ron Shoesmith, the director of the city archaeology unit, who has kindly given his consent.

I am very grateful to the City Museum Staff, especially Peter Young, Catherine Willson and Bob Gennard, who have kindly allowed me to search through the whole of their print collection and use those pictures I thought would be of interest to readers of this book.

The old photographs used in this volume are mainly reproduced from old picture postcards, some of which are in poor condition, but because of the historical interest have been included in this book.

I am always interested to hear from any reader who has, or knows of, any similar photographs which I can copy for possible future use.

Permission to reproduce photographs has been sought from all possible sources, but in a few cases contact could not be made with the copyright holders, so the author apologises to them. All pictures reproduced remain the copyright of the original owners.

Derek Foxton
November 1997

Acknowledgements

This book would not have been possible without the help of so many people who have granted me access to photographs and given permission to reproduce them. I would like to thank the following:-

The Dean and Chapter of Hereford; Miss J. Williams and the Mappa Mundi Trust; the Royal Photographic Society; the Museum department of the Hereford City Council; Robin Hill of the City Reference Library; Sue Hubbard and her staff at the County Records Office; Dave Rogers of Welsh Water; Mr. N. Pigott of the Hereford Fire Brigade; Mike Davies of M. D. Helicopters, Lower Bullingham; Ron Shoesmith of the Hereford City Archeological Unit; Mr. M. Fowler the Headmaster of St. James' School; Colin Petts and George Thomas at H. P. Bulmer; Harold Haines, David Hales, Mr. & Mrs. Wilfred Charles, Miss Mary Banton, Miss Jean Banton, Rev. Andrew Mottram, Hampton Grange Nursing Home, Mr. Alan Edmunds, Mr. S. Sockett, Mr. & Mrs. Heijn, Mr. P. Teague, Ken & Gareth Lewis, Mrs. Prowlin, Jack Thomas, Ted Hadley, Stewart Gilbert the Editor of the Hereford Times, Mr. Skinner and his granddaughter Samantha, Rev. Robert Harris, Mr. H. R. Wood, Mr. M. Rooke, Mr. Lane, Mr. Roy Blackler, Jane Denny, Eddie Powell, Peter Dean, Tom Parfitt, Peter Wright, the late Percy Pritchard A.R.P.S., Mrs. Susie Major, R. H. H. Barneby, Barbara Rhys, Mr. Tomlinson and of course Basil Butcher.

Without the help of my wife Maria this book would not have been published. Dennis Eagles was a great help with his advice on setting up a new computer system and I would also like to thank Heather Jason who advised me on the use of all the computer software.

Finally a thank you to David Postle who designed the dust jacket at very short notice.

This unusual picture of the Cathedral was taken from the city Museum about 1914. The shop on the left sold Art and Needlework equipment, then there was a boarding house, owned by Walter Pritchard and the third shop was a saddlers called James. At the far end was another boarding house run by Mrs. Carless.

The whole row of houses was demolished in 1935 transforming the view of the Cathedral.

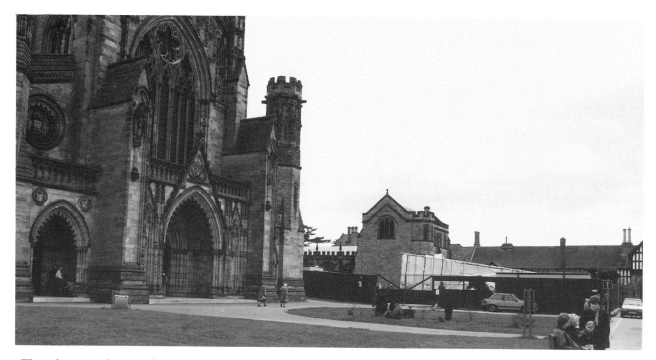

This photograph was taken during excavations on the site of the proposed Mappa Mundi and Chained Library building. The whole area of the Cathedral Close was for many centuries the city burial ground. There is a temporary structure over the excavation area to provide protection from the weather. The west front of the Cathedral was rebuilt early this century and dedicated by the Archbishop of Canterbury on April 26th 1905. The Dean Leigh Library, in the centre of this photograph, was built in 1897 as a library for Cathedral books and archives.

The Mappa Mundi building, which houses the old map and Chained Library was officially opened by H.R.H. Queen Elizabeth II and the Duke of Edinburgh on May 3rd 1996. Building work began in September 1994 using Derbyshire stone for the external walls to match the adjacent Dean Leigh Library. The roof is supported by 'A-frame' oak trusses, which are a feature of the reading library. A sophisticated system controls the air quality, humidity, temperature, fire alarm and fire extinguishers. The building has recently been awarded the Royal Fine Art Commission's 'Building of the Year 1997' which is one of the top national architecture awards.

This Victorian photograph of the Archdeacon's house at the south end of Church Street was taken from near the Cathedral. The tall building is 18th century and listed grade 2. Inside is a dogleg staircase with turned balusters and the cellar is of brick and stone. The corner building is much older and has a timber frame construction.

It is very interesting to compare this picture with the early one. The extension is a perfect match to the original half.

In Hereford Cathedral there used to be a wrought iron screen in front of the chancel which stood between the eastern pillars of the tower. It was an elaborate example of artistic metal work made by Skidmore of Coventry from designs by Sir Gilbert Scott. The screen was decorated by a variety of foliage and flowers made from thin plates of copper and hammered iron. The central arch was surmounted by a richly jewelled cross and the design included seven bronze figures.

The view from the nave towards the altar is now unobstructed giving a more open feel to the Cathedral. In recent years a raised dais was built under the tower on which was placed a new altar and altar rails. The idea was to give the congregation a better chance of seeing and feeling more a part of the service. The former Bishop of Hereford, John Eastaugh, had a vision of creating some sort of 'Majestas' to give people a feeling of hope and joy in the resurrection and the descending power of the Holy Spirit, so Simon Beer was commissioned to build a corona, which now hangs suspended over the altar. The corona was dedicated on December 5th 1992, to the late Bishop's sixteen year episcopate.

Books have been kept in the cathedral from the earliest days, when they were hand-written on vellum and highly treasured. They were stored in chests like the one on the right of the picture, which dates from the 14th century, and had 3 locks, each requiring a different key. In 1590 the books were moved into the Lady Chapel. In 1611 the stall system was built by Richard Rogers of Hereford and the ironwork and chains made in Oxford. This photograph was taken soon after 1855 when some of the cases were moved to a room over the North Transept aisle, but poorly reassembled. In 1897 the remaining part of the Library was installed in the newly built Dean Leigh building.

The complete chained library has now been installed in the new purpose built Mappa Mundi building, paid for by the National Heritage Memorial Fund and John Paul Getty Junior. The building has a very secure storage vault, ground floor display area and on the top floor there is the cathedral reference library and reading room. *Photograph reproduced with kind permission of the Dean and Chapter of Hereford and Mappa Mundi Trust.*

This rare photograph shows the houses that used to stand in Cathedral Close being demolished, with the wall of the house belonging to Mrs. Lizzie Carless just starting to fall down. The cathedral west front is to the right of the picture. *Photograph reproduced by kind permission of the late Percy Pritchard A.R.P.S.*

The demolition of the former houses has opened up the area around the cathedral and improved the view from King Street and Broad Street.

Palace Yard, which is opposite the west front of the Cathedral, has one of the most interesting views in the centre of Hereford. This photograph taken by Peter Dean about 1970 shows a jumble of tin roof buildings, his house and studio which were owned for well over 100 years by the Bustin family of photographers who were very well known in their day. Note the photographic display units on the wall of the house.

During the early 1990's the old sheds were removed and these rather attractive houses built.

This superb Victorian photograph is of a horse drawn omnibus in High Town. The service which ran from the railway station to Whitecross was provided by Connelly's who were coach manufacturers in Commercial Road. This photograph is reproduced by kind permission of Mrs. Susie Major in memory of her late husband who owned the Skeffington Hume Dodgson (brother of Lewis Carroll) collection of Herefordshire photographs.

Since pedestrianisation buses are no longer seen in High Town.

This is one of the earliest dated photographs showing The Old House with a glimpse into Commercial Street and St. Peter's Street. The Old House which was built c.1621 was once part of a row of houses called Butchers Row which was demolished about 1825. The porch has ornately decorated posts, lintel, brackets and barge-boards.

The Old House is now one of the city's most visited attractions.

This is the only known photograph of the Old Market Hall built c.1575, which was taken in 1855, six years before its demolition. The building can be seen to the left of the Old House and here it is covered in stucco and has been completely altered since it was built. Nicholas Pevsner described the original thus; "It was the most fantastic black and white building imaginable." It is interesting to see the early gas lamp on the right. *Photograph reproduced by courtesy of the Royal Photographic Society.*

The end of the Old House had windows inserted when it was restored by Lloyds Bank shortly after they purchased it in the 1880's. Some of the distant buildings have been replaced.

Here the manager of Adams, a shop which was in High Town, poses for the camera. The shop and its advertisements are well lit by 3 large gas lamps and the window is full of pictures, postcards, toys, stationery and gifts. On the first floor is some stained glass. To the right is Stead and Simpson and to the left Boots the chemist. The entrance to Church Street is illuminated by a gas lamp.

Today the premises are occupied by a business selling take-away lunches and snacks, but the shop front has not altered since the 1950's.

Motor vehicles began to appear in Hereford from the turn of the century and as they became more reliable they sold in larger numbers. By 1912 when this photograph was taken, motorcars were a regular sight, though most long distance journeys were still by rail and local transport was mostly horse-drawn. The cars seen here are on the north side of High Town and motor historian David Hales identifies the vehicles as follows:– from the left a Landaulet taxi, a Wolseley Siddeley registered in Cardiff, another Wolseley registered in Hereford, a Darracq owned by The Hereford Motor Company, and a Clement Talbot. It is worth noting the oil and acetylene lamps and the flags. The shops from the extreme left are as follows:– Kings Acre Nurseries Ltd, The Popular Cafe, Ralph Clark Chemists, Jakeman & Carver booksellers, and Walmsley a drapers. *Photograph reproduced by kind permission of Harold Haines.*

Some of the old buildings survive but sadly most of the shop fronts have gone. The pedestrianisation of High Town has ensured that it remains traffic free.

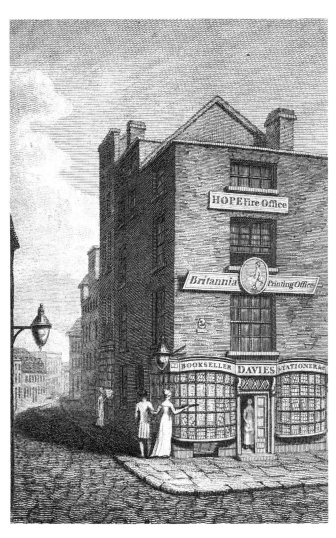

This is an engraving on a postcard of the shop on the corner of High Town and Widemarsh Street where in 1858 T. T. Davis was listed as a bookseller. In 1914 the shop was owned by Kings Acre Nurseries and by 1922 Bell & Company had become tobacconists there. It is interesting to see the fire mark on the wall.

The upper windows are the same as on the engraving but the shop windows have been changed and extended along Widemarsh Street.

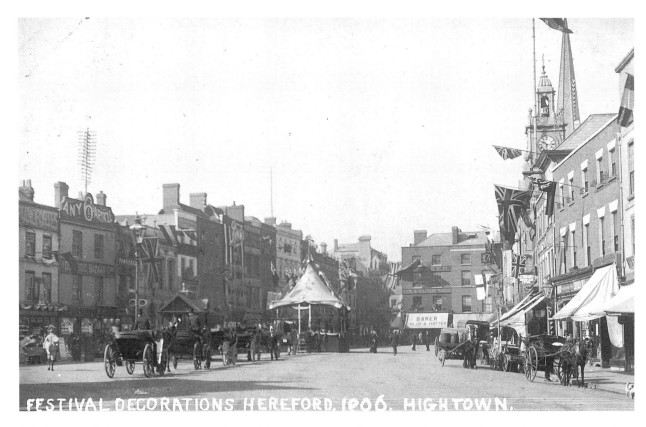

FESTIVAL DECORATIONS HEREFORD. 1906. HIGHTOWN.

The Hereford Corporation made a huge effort to decorate the city for the 1906 Three Choirs Festival. This is a general view across High Town which shows the bandstand they erected. To the right is the Market Hall clock and All Saints Church spire. The small hut to the left of the bandstand was the cabbies' shelter, hay store, and tea room. There are five cabs waiting for their fares. The tall telegraph pole is where the city telephone exchange was. On the left of the picture the pipe organ attached to the wall belonged to William Mason, a music warehouse owner. The High Town Post Office was also here. At the far end of High Town on the corner of High Street, is Baker's, a tailoring shop.

Over recent years the trees have grown and during hot, sunny weather provide some shade for pedestrians.

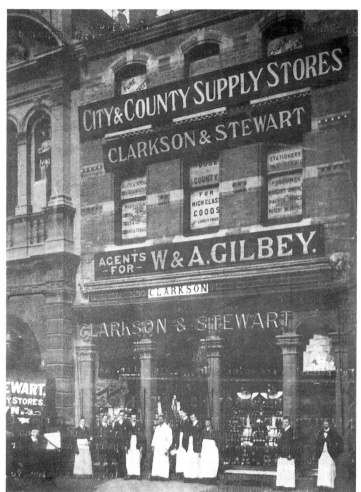

At the turn of the century there were two large grocery shops on the north side of High Town. This photograph, taken in 1908 is of Clarkson & Stewart who were next door to the Market Hall. They claimed that they were second to none in quality and superior to most in actual value. By 1925 this shop was owned by Fearis & Co., a name still remembered by many Herefordians.

The upper foors of the original building survive although the brick has been painted over.

Although this is a much photographed view of Hereford this particular picture is of special interest because not only does it have a boat in full sail but it also shows the only paddle steamer ever to visit the city, in about 1886 – 1889. Note the earlier front of the Cathedral *(Hereford Then & Now Volume 2, page 7.)*

The river is now not used as much as it used to be. It is classified as a 'Site of Special Scientific Interest' which means that any future developments along the banks are carefully controlled.

For many centuries the Wye was used as a major route from the south into Hereford but only when the river level was high. This view is of the north end of the old bridge with an assortment of buildings including Wye Terrace on the far side. The terraced houses to the right were approached from Gwynne Street and were liable to regular flooding. The bridge was built in the late 15th century with six arches and widened in 1826.

This photograph was taken in September 1997.

This is a computer generated picture of the proposed development which has just received planning permission. *Reproduced by kind permission of Mr. & Mrs. Heijn.*

The focal point of this photograph is All Saints' Church which is at the far end of Broad Street. This picture taken before 1874 is the only one known that shows the old building on the site of the City Museum and Library seen here behind the lamp post on the left. It was a tea, coffee, wine and spirits shop called Hewitt. Soon after this photograph was taken the shop was demolished to make way for the City Museum and Library.

The Museum and Library building was opened on October 8th 1874 with two small shops at the front which were a tobacconist and a haberdasher. The building cost £7,600 of which £6,100 was given by Sir James Rankin and £1,500 by the Corporation. It was built of brick and stone with a profusion of carvings mainly of animals. The new buildings next door are an example of 1960's architecture, but completely out of character for the street.

The photographer has used a long time exposure for this picture taken in 1909. All Saints' Church spire and tower dominate the view. In 1885 the spire was renovated at a cost of £1,700 and several influential citizens were allowed up to the top of the scaffolding. Further restoration schemes were undertaken in 1893 and 1903. The church was built in the early English decorated and perpendicular styles with a spire 240 feet high and 8 bells in the tower. The White Hart Wine Vaults is to the left of the photograph with the United Counties Bank Ltd. next door. The entrance into West Street is just visible and on the far side of the junction is the Kings' Head Hotel with its round turret.

The attractive stone faced corner of The Kings Head Hotel has been replaced with a modern 1960's building. By 1993 All Saints Church spire had become dangerous and restoration was urgently needed. The top 72 feet of the spire were removed, then rebuilt using original stones for the first 12 feet and new stone for the rest. This was part of a £1.8 million restoration and modernisation scheme completed in July 1997.

FESTIVAL DECORATIONS - BROAD ST.   F. PREECE. PHOTO.

Hereford is host city to the Three Choirs Festival once every three years. This view looking south along Broad Street was taken in 1906 when the City Corporation provided very lavish street decorations for the Festival. This structure represented the Victoria Bridge and was one of several erected in the city. To the left is The Queen's Arms Public House owned by James Deen and on the right is the Birmingham & Counties Banking Company Ltd. whose manager, at that time, was Charles Morris Armitage. This later became Barclays Bank before it moved across the road to its present site. The Green Dragon Hotel can be seen behind the central bridge support. Its facade dates from 1857 but the roof, which can be seen on aerial photographs, reveals that the listed grade 2 building was once a row of five houses. Just visible at the far end of Broad Street in the centre of the road is the cabbies' tea hut.

Hereford has not seen such lavish street decorations since then. Some of the old buildings have gone and their replacements do not do our City any justice.

27

Many museums of the last century were very static, often overcrowded, giving very little information and were of poor educational value. This photograph reveals that this was so in the local museum in Broad Street c. 1930, which was in a large purpose built gallery on the first floor above the City Library. There was certainly a great deal to look at; bird eggs, stuffed birds and animals, butterflies, moths, geological fossils, some local antiquities, mainly Roman and two early cycles, but these exhibits were poorly arranged. *Photograph is reproduced with kind permission of The City Museum.*

During 1997 the Museum has been undergoing some major changes. This will enable the visitors to enjoy and understand the exhibits.

For centuries Herefordshire's main industry was farming. This 1915 photograph was taken of the Corn Exchange in Broad Street when motor vehicles were relatively uncommon and the horse drawn cart was used for most work. This coal cart owned by Cope and Baker is outside their head office. The building on the left is the Kemble Theatre and in the window of the Corn Exchange is a board for James Taylor, an architect and surveyor. The main building in this picture is the Hop Market which contains many small offices. The names which are legible on the brass plates are Wheeler Meats, accountants, Edwards & Armstrong, electrical and mechanical machinery engineers and Sydney Myer & Co., In the window are three baskets of coal.

This is one building in the City which does not enhance the general street scene.

The Five Ways Inn, a Victorian beer house, which had a ground floor 16 feet wide and 52 feet long stood on the corner of Commercial Street and Maylord Street. There are eleven wooden beer barrels on the pavement which indicates a large consumption by customers.

By 1934 the building was being used by T. Morgan and Son, who were butchers and later in 1968 it was demolished as part of a road widening scheme for the Inner City Relief Road. The replacement structure was erected in 1985.

Hereford had several almshouses and hospitals for the elderly and the poor. This photograph was taken about 25 years ago of Trinity or Kerry's Hospital in Commercial Street which was founded by Sir Thomas Kerry of Sheffield Court, Kent about 1600 for 3 unmarried men and 13 poor widows who were nominated by the Mayor and citizens of Hereford. The building in the photograph was erected in 1825 and cost £880. There was an identical row opposite which formed a courtyard.

The buildings were demolished by the City Council as part of a major redevelopment. The old metal gate and fence now stand near St. Giles' Chapel in St Owen Street.

This tree-lined street is Commercial Road about 1905. The road is two steps below the pavement which seems to have a soft surface. The large building to the left is Greenlands' new furniture warehouse built in 1899. The brick front is a fine specimen of late Victorian design. The large wall advertisement reads; "Competitive prices – removal contractors – continental removers – estimates free – special staff of expert packers – safety guaranteed." Next door is a large sign for Bethell's which was a confectioner's shop. The far shop with the curved name fascia is Portlock's the bootmakers. The tall church turrets of the Baptist Church can be seen above the roof line and in the distance a driver of a horse-drawn carriage is wearing a top hat.

Today the City Council does not approve of the centuries old tradition of painting large advertisements on buildings. Note the extension to the old Greenlands building.

This is the Hereford Baptist Church in Commercial Road with its fine stone front and Norman style arches. The twin towers give a solid look to the structure. This is the second Baptist Church in the road. The original church stood some 60 yards further east and had a graveyard. The foundation stone for the new church was laid in June 1837 and opened on Good Friday, April 13th 1838, built at a cost of under £1,000. This photograph of a military parade was taken about 1950.

The Church has been renovated in recent years. Note the alterations to the towers.

Commercial Road, one of the major roads into the city, had many inns and hotels, among them the Merton Hotel, which was near the railway station. According to Ron Shoesmith, who researched inns and public houses of Hereford, the hotel was first mentioned in 1863. A bill headed 1893, advertised that it was a general posting house, supplying funerals and had its own omnibus to take guests to the railway station. An old receipt shows that a dog cart ride to Pontrilas district cost £1. This picture postcard shows the front of the hotel and was posted in 1908 when the landlord was Edward Foster.

This present day photograph shows the extensive alterations made to the front of the building.

This is the shop of Franklin Barnes at 4 Commercial Road about 1909. In 1914 an advertisement proclaimed that they "sold grain, seeds of all sorts, forage for horses, stuffs of all kinds" and that they manufactured their own animal feeds in a large warehouse behind the shop. They were also contractors to H.M. Government and the Army and had another shop in Bridge Street which was their head-office. Mr. Barnes is seen here between two of his employees.

The business survived until 1994. In the 1930's the shop was completely rebuilt then in the late 1960's the present corner building was erected.

The Hereford Trade Directory of 1890 lists over fifty bootmakers. This photograph taken about 1910 shows John Henry Portlock in a white apron outside his shop at 61 Commercial Road. He is holding a new boot, which has four rows of nails on the sole. There is a reflection in the window which reads T. Vale, who was a boot repairer at No. 16. The shop to the left is Magness and Son a florists.

Commercial Road now shows the growth of fast food outlets.

This picture of the May Fair in Commercial Road was taken in about 1955. In the foreground is Commercial Square with a small roundabout. Blueschool Street is to the left where the Black and White Café was owned by H. Powell and the Sanitary Laundry had an enormous painted advertisement above the shop. The white building next door is Franklin Barnes and the chimney is at Monkmoor Mills opposite the bus station. In those days the fair spread along the road as far as the cinema.

Since the inner ring road was built, all the buildings on the left of the old photograph have gone. The modern corner building is Franklin House, which has several shop units on the ground floor and offices above.

The old City Jail, designed by the famous architect Nash, was built in Commercial Road near the railway station on the site of St Guthlac's Priory at a cost of £16,646 and in 1902 it was enlarged and improved. This photograph was taken just before it was demolished about 1932. The sign above the entrance invites the public to have a look inside at a cost of sixpence.

The present building opened as the Ritz cinema on January 10th 1938. Wilfred Southworth played the Compton Organ before the opening film "Maytime" was shown. The organ was later sold in 1967 after having stood unused for some time. In 1972 the Cinema was divided into two parts, one half became a Bingo Club and the other half a new cinema with 378 seats.. Then in the 1980's the Bingo Club was closed and the premises re-opened as a night club, which at present is called 'Marilyn's'.

This photograph of Church Street was taken from the top of the Cathedral tower. The Archdeacon's House is prominent at the front of the picture and the pale roof behind is 20 Church Street, a very early timber framed house which dates back to about 1400. Its uneven roof line indicates that there is probably extensive structural damage. To the right is a long garden which extends to the rear of the Conservative Club and in the lower left corner is Arthur Virgo, a monumental mason. The long roof behind the pyramidal roof is St. John Baptist School where Mrs. Harris was headmistress.

The biggest change to be seen on the lower left of this recent picture is the building of a telephone exchange for the city during the 1950's. Today it is no longer used for this purpose as all calls now go through the exchange at Barton Road. The building was recently purchased by the Hereford Cathedral School and will provide it with much needed space.

At the turn of the century there were 49 bootmakers in Hereford including Stead & Simpson. This is a photograph of Thomas Vale (centre) with his staff outside the shop at 14 Church Street taken in November 1910. At this time there were other members of the Vale family working as bootmakers, one at 13 King Street, another at 123 St. Owen Street and Thomas with his shops at 31a Eign Street, Commercial Road and Church Street.

During the research for this picture it was a surprise to find that most of the original shop front is still there in a remarkable state of preservation. In 1995 the whole of the front of this building was exposed during some restoration work and it was found that the original timber frame was badly damaged so had to be covered with stucco. Mr. Skinner and his granddaughter Samantha are in the entrance to the shop.

This is a photograph taken in 1909 of St Owen's School which opened in 1905 and was built to the latest designs, with a large central assembly hall and classrooms on either side. It was heated by a large bore cast iron central heating system. High on the wall in the hall were two foot prints which showed the boys how to stand.

The building is still used for educational purposes by the County Council Social Services Department as a centre for disabled adults. The extensive alterations to the original building can be seen.

Market day in Hereford has always been on a Wednesday when cattle were driven into town on the hoof early in the day. This photograph taken in 1902 is of Mr Llewellyn, a saddler, whose main shop was in Union Street. He has just set up his display which consists of a wide range of equine goods, garden forks and hop twine. The buildings in the background are in Newmarket Street and the sign "The Globe Inn" is just visible behind the Llewellyn fascia. The Globe Inn ceased trading on September 30th 1932 when Sunderland's moved in. On the extreme right edge of the picture is The Wheatsheaf Hotel. On the large advertisement board is the name J. & R. Miller who had a business in Widemarsh Street.

At the Cattle Market today sheep pens cover the site of the old photograph. Large buildings, including the covered market area, obscure the distant view.

The 1914 Hereford Trades Directory lists Llewellyn & Co., Saddlers at 36 and 38 Blueschool Street. This rare photograph shows the shop with its staff.

The site today is now part of the Inner Relief Road.

On December 18th 1821 the Town Commissars decided against converting to gas to light the city as it was no cheaper than the oil they were using, but by 1826 the streets were all lit by gas lamps. This photograph is of the Electricity Generating Station which stood in Widemarsh Street behind where the multi-story car park now stands. It was opened on December 14th 1899 by the Mayor, Councillor Edward Bosley. The motive power for the generators was produced by 2 Belliss steam engines and cables were laid across the inner city as far as the old gates. The chimney which is nearest to the camera was 85 feet high.

Today there is still a transformer building in the corner of the Cattle Market car park.

For the first forty years of this century this building was the store and workshop for Bowers, a large building company. This photograph of their large workshop was taken about 1935 in Bath Street and the road leading away from the camera to the back of the Shire Hall was Delacy Street.

In 1939 the building was used by the Fire Brigade to store their equipment. By 1955 the premises had become a garage called Byford Motor Engineers and then finally, Godsells Garage.

In May 1997 the buildings were demolished and the site cleared to make way for a car park.

The Working Boys Home in Bath Street was established in 1874 by a committee of gentlemen to receive boys aged 9-14 who were either orphans or growing up destitute. They were clothed and fed, taught gardening, farming, shoemaking and basketry and eventually employment would be found for them. They were also taught music and played for festive occasions in the City. While at the home they were expected to help out with domestic chores.

Over the years the building has been extended by the addition of a chapel and various offices. The old County Council was based here as well as in the Shire Hall. Today the chapel is used as the City Registry Office.

Fire fighting in the county was the responsibility of the local police force for the first 40 years of this century so the Chief Constable was also the Chief Fire Officer. The fire engine garage was in De Lacy Street which was adjacent to the police station in Gaol Street. (*see Hereford Then & Now Volume 2 page 38*). The buildings in De Lacy Street were built in 1884 to house members of the police force and their families. Since the fire crews were made up of the policemen who lived there, an emergency fire crew could be quickly called. This photograph of the Herefordshire Fire Brigade in 1927 shows the Merryweather fire tender on the left with some other appliances . The tall man standing on the Merryweather is police Sgt. Hadley and Chief Constable T. Rawson is standing in the centre.

Today the old fire station has gone and the site is now a police car park. There are two modern fire tenders with their crews who are as follows:– from the left, Fire Fighter David Iles, Sub Officer Neil Piggott, Leading Fire Fighter Nicholas Wiggin and Fire Fighters Peter Green, Ian Fox, Andrew Symonds, Nick Sumner, David Walker and Amanda Gillard.

It was a wet day on June 11th 1896 when the foundation stone was laid by Mrs Bather for the new school at St. James. The school was endowed by public subscription for the Parish of St. James. The scaffolding has been put to good use to fly the flags. The chairs are on wooden boards and St. James Church can be seen on the right.

The school celebrated its centenary on June 12th 1996 when the Mayor and MayoressCouncillors Les and Sue Andrews paid a visit. This picture shows the large crowd, with the pupils dressed in Victorian costumes. A time capsule was buried and a plaque unveiled.

In 1905 Hereford had four Temperance Hotels. There were three in Commercial Road and Commercial Street, while this one was in Widemarsh Street. The photographer, Mr Edwin Sledmere, had a problem since he could not include in his picture the full height of the building, which was unusually high for Hereford, possibly the tallest that was inhabited. The owner Walter Doubleday made use of the ground floor as his dining and coffee room. The gas lamp is on the Bulmer's wine and spirits shop on the corner of Bewell Street.

It is possible that the architect of this building made an error in the design since the upper floors have been removed. The hotel business ceased long ago and the street lamps are now all electric.

At the turn of the century this house in Widemarsh Street was used as the offices for the City Corporation. It was built as a home for Dr. Brewster soon after he came to Hereford in 1697. He was a local doctor and a collector of valuable books and when he died in 1715 he bequeathed most of his books to his old college in Oxford and the remainder to All Saints Church.

The house was altered in 1907 when the ground floor was converted into two shops with an archway in the middle. The left shop was owned by Sydney Wright who specialised in farm produce, while next door was Jenkins a tailor.

The original house is now one large shop still divided by the central arch which has become a passageway to Tesco's car park and store.

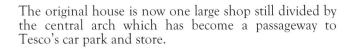

The Red Lion Inn, which was a half-timbered building that had been stuccoed, stood at the junction of Eign Street and Victoria Street. It was demolished in June 1900. The Red Lion landlady's husband was Charles Cox who is seen in this photograph below the gas lamp with his arms folded. Charles was a pattern maker and not interested in the pub which was run by his wife. At the rear of the inn was a large stable yard which was always full on market days. The delivery cart has the name F. Whalen on it and the corner post on the left belongs to Kings, monumental masons.

The new Red Lion was opened in 1908 as a 14 bedroom hotel with extensive new stables in the yard. It was built in the mock Tudor style on the upper floor with brick below.

This block of 22 residential flats was built in 1978.

Hereford was the hub of a large railway network in the county. There were goods yards near the station at Barrs Court and near the earlier station at Barton. This level crossing was in Edgar Street, over the line that took trains into the Cattle Market and the Electricity Generating Station. This photograph is of the Moorfields area with the refuse disposal plant chimney visible in the distance. The road on the left is Canonmoor Street and just behind the houses was a large corporation car park.

The Salvation Army have transformed this corner of the city with a new Citadel, an award winning building, which is one of the best designed modern structures in the city. The railway lines have gone and the whole area has been redeveloped with various housing schemes.

The south end of Edgar Street used to be quite narrow with many buildings in a poor state of repair because they had been scheduled for demolition to make way for the Inner Relief Road. The name on the left shop is Foster & Skeffington, top class photographers, who later moved to a prestigious site in High Town. Next door was P. J. Lewis, motor cycle repairers and then T. Clark & Son furniture dealers. The half-timbered building in the distance is the Red Lion Hotel. To the right is a branch of Jessons Stores.

This site is now the busiest road junction in the city.

This picture postcard of the Aylestone Hill Toll Gate, with the photographer's horse-drawn dark-room, was posted in July 1906. It was taken on the top of the hill near the Venns Lane junction by Ladmore of 17 King Street, who advertised in 1876 that he took photographs of every description – portraits, landscapes, architectural views etc. This photograph was taken before 1870 when tolls were abolished.

The road has now been widened and there is no visible evidence of the old Toll House.

Just outside the city boundary along the Worcester Road is the Lugg Bridge Mill. This late Victorian photograph shows the complete range of buildings over the river and along the bank. The mill buildings, erected in 1811 by Richard Prince were seven storeys high had two under-shot wheels driving seven pairs of stones. There was a wharf where Forest of Dean coal was sold and a lock for barges to the left, though navigation was always precarious. By 1870 the ownership of the mill had passed to the Brain family and in 1925 they sold out to the River Lugg Drainage Board. The mills were thought to have been the largest of their kind in Britain. *This photograph is reproduced with the kind permission of Basil Butcher.*

The river board cleared the Weir, demolished the dilapidated buildings across the river and the ancient Lugg Bridge was once again exposed to view. In 1983 there was a planning application to remove the upper floor and convert the building into a restaurant. The present owner Mr Lane is restoring and converting the remaining buildings into several flats.

The college in College Road was built in 1880 at a cost of £17,000 and was called The County College which was a boys' school with grounds of 6½ acres. It was not a financial success so the buildings were sold to the Council Education Committee in 1903 who established a Training College for elementary school mistresses. This is a photograph of the first principle Miss Sophie Smith with her staff and pupils outside the main entrance in 1905.

The buildings are now occupied by the Royal National College for the Blind who moved in on October 1978 from their former premises in Shropshire. This photograph, taken by the Hereford Times, is of the Archbishop of Canterbury and his wife, being greeted by the principal Dr. Colin Housby-Smith accompanied by the Bishop of Hereford and his wife Mrs. Oliver during their visit in June 1997 which is the 125th year of the R.N.C.B. *This photograph is reproduced by courtesy of the Hereford Times.*

The railways into Hereford were constructed by different companies. The line from Newport to Barton Station was opened on January 2nd 1854,. the Shrewsbury line into Barrs Court opened on December 6th 1853 and the Gloucester line in September 1861. This photograph, taken from Newtown Road railway bridge before 1915, shows the extensive sidings and unloading areas with goods and engine sheds on either side of the signal gantry supports. The Station is just visible in the far distance.

The railway track in the sidings is now almost disused and has become very rusty. There are plans to remove most of the remaining lines and possibly redevelop the land.

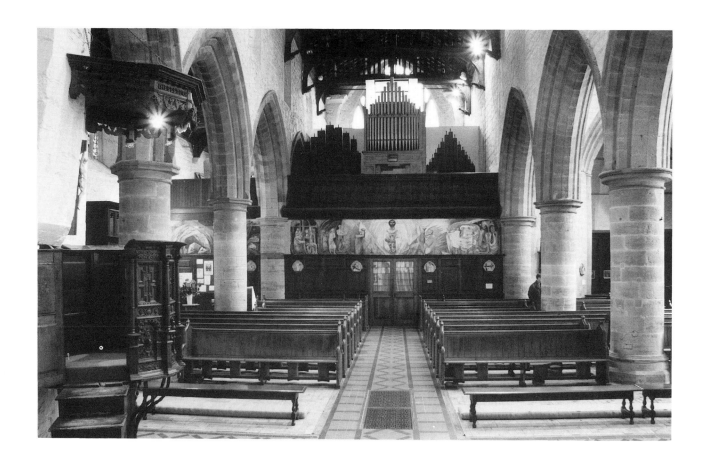

On the left of this interior view of All Saints Church is the pulpit, which is of Flemish design and execution, has 6 beautiful carved panels and is surrounded by tracery work. It was made in 1621 and cost £7. At the far end is the gallery in front of the west window. The organ was installed in 1826 when the church was enlarged to increase the number of seats to 500.

After 5 years of restoration and modernisation work the church re-opened in July 1997 with a restaurant, ultra modern kitchen, vestry, toilets and office. The organ and font have been relocated. It has now become a favourite lunch venue for many people with its friendly atmosphere and excellent food.

This old postcard view of the interior of All Saints Church dated 19th September 1920, is of the chancel taken from the west door. The chancel roof has original 'barrel-work' in oak timber and was restored in 1981. A plaque on the wall commemerates David Garrick, the great English actor who was baptised here. The altar table is Jacobean, dated about 1620.

Following recent restorations the west end of the church is now a thriving restaurant run by Bill Sewell from London. The design by Rod Robinson Associates is an ingenious blend of old with new and the modern structure stands on rubber tipped legs, which means that the whole kitchen and restaurant area can be removed without a mark being left on the old church building. The 15th century chancel wall painting was restored in the 1960's and is just visible in the picture.

Carton Work Class-Juniors. Blue Coat School. Hereford.

Early photographs taken inside a school room in Hereford are extremely rare. This was taken inside the Bluecool School which was in Blueschool Street near Commercial Square. It was founded in 1710 and the present red-brick building erected in 1827 had a maximum capacity for 378 pupils but 420 were registered. In 1910 the school was remodelled to accommodate 450 children. The average attendance for boys and girls was 334 days per year. By 1922 it had become a girls' school under the headship of Miss Marsh. The picture shows how regimented the classes were.

In the late 1960's the girls' school closed and most of the pupils and teachers were moved to the old girls' High School in Coningsby Street. The building was then used as a factory manufacturing windows and conservatories. In 1997 the firm relocated and the present picture shows the old equipment just before clearance. It was difficult to locate the exact spot where the old photograph was taken because the interior had been extensively rebuilt.

60

This postcard view is of the New Harp Inn, in Union Street. To the left is the entrance into Gaol Street where part of the White Horse Hotel can be seen. According to Shoesmith the first recorded inn on this site was The Union in 1862 with Charles Field the landlord. By 1876 The Union had been re-named The New Harp. Shoesmith records that the Inn was on a middle plot between Gaol Street and another tavern The Flower Pot. However the picture confirms that the inn consists of two adjacent houses that probably had the internal walls removed. The year is 1907.

The original building has been replaced and has had further extensive renovations done in 1995 and since renamed Oscars. The White Horse Hotel has been demolished.

In 1929 R. J. Wood was recorded as trading as a clothier at 3a Union Street and this photograph was taken outside his shop with his shop assistants. By 1934 he was also listed as a furniture dealer and he had a motor engineering and auto services business in his stable yard. The bicycle looks like a recent purchase.

The present building was erected during the 1930's where there is now a charity shop and a garage business still survives.

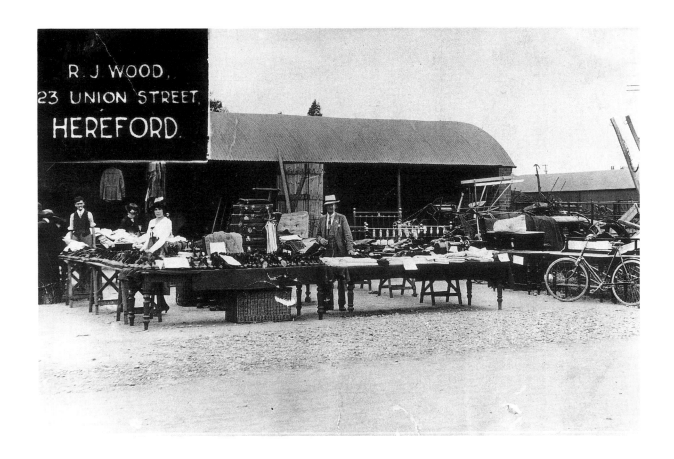

While he ran his main business in Union Street, Mr. Wood would set up a stall at the Wednesday Cattle Market selling boots, shoes and clothes on long tables with turned legs.

Today this corner of the market has a permanent building and the traders market area is just a short distance away.

Moreton on Lugg is only a short distance away from Hereford. Moreton Court was built on the site of an old mansion house soon after Thomas Evans purchased the land in 1864. The architect was Mr J. H. Knight of Cheltenham. The house was described as an elegant mansion in the Italian Elizabethan style and was 'L' shaped with a stone tower. This photograph was taken about 1914 when its owner was Mrs Hill, the lady of the manor. The last owner who lived here was Joseph Counsell, chairman of United Diaries, who purchased the building in 1935.

The house was demolished in 1958. During the last war the nearby Moreton Camp was built as an American distribution depot, while the house was used for the soldiers accommodation. Today the position of the old house is hidden from view by all the recent buildings.

In Medieval times Hereford had several monasteries and the Coningsby Hospital was built near the site of the Blackfriars' monastery in Widemarsh Street by Sir Thomas Coningsby of Hampton Court, Bodenham, who added three sides to the much older building of the Knights' Templars. The hospital had accommodation for 12 aged soldiers and their wives, a fine chapel and dining room. The monastic remains and an ancient preaching cross can still be seen behind the hospital. This photograph, taken early this century is of the elderly residents enjoying the afternoon sun. Note the poor road surface.

The exterior of the hospital was restored during a major rebuilding operation a few years ago. St. Thomas Cantilupe Junior School is on the far side of the hospital. There is now a museum next to the Chapel which is open to visitors several afternoons a week.

This picture of a line-up of smartly dressed men near the charabanc was taken outside the Race Horse Inn, Newtown Road, probably about 1914, when the landlord was John Cooke. The stable yard was through the archway.

The new building was erected by Bevan and Hodges in 1938. A large car park replaces the coach houses, stables and yard.

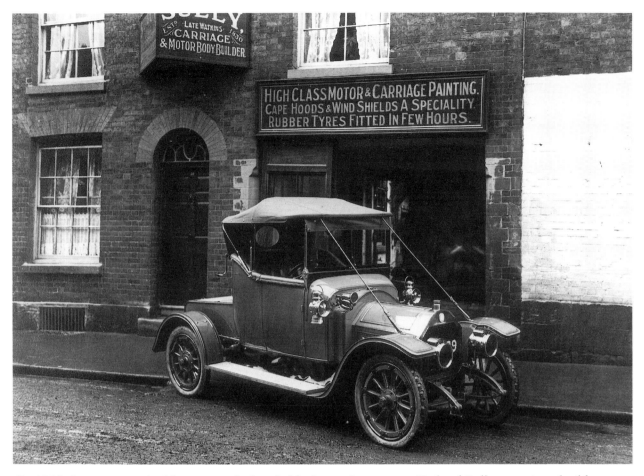

By 1912 the motor car had become a fairly reliable form of transport. Richard Sully, a carriage builder, was prosperous enough to purchase this car, seen here outside his works in Bridge Street, adjacent to the corner of Gwynne Street, where the main entrance was. This car, thought to be a Scout, was made in Salisbury and registered as C J 1159 in Hereford on July 29th 1912. It was described as a 4 cylinder, three seater, painted in grey. The previous owner of the business, John Watkins, was recorded as a coach builder in 1876.

The picture today is a sad sight but there are now extensive plans to develop a large riverside restaurant, which should be completed in 1999.

In 1929 The Black Lion in Bridge Street was run by Thomas Rooke and this picture was taken shortly after he had moved in with his family. There was a large yard at the rear where The Midland Red bus company had their depot. The hanging sign on the left reads – 'Booking Office, Midland Red Motor Tours.'

Before restoration Basil Butcher mentioned to the owners that the original timbers would be under the stucco. The building has been fully renovated , the stucco removed and the original timbers exposed.

This church, set back on the east side of Bridge Street was the Wesleyan Methodist Chapel. The Hereford Wesleyan Society was established in a cottage near the Wye Bridge; their first church opened in 1829 and in 1868 it was enlarged to seat 380. The shop to the right was the Cae-Glas 'snack-bar'.

The chapel, which is no longer used for worship, is now no longer visible from the street. It was sold and new shops built adjacent to the pavement.

Until the early 1950's Hunderton Farm, which stands on a high bank above the River Wye, was approached from Hunderton Road by way of a ford over the Newtown Brook. The house is in the Clehonger parish but the City boundary follows the brook which is adjacent to the farm buildings. This photograph was taken in the 1920's when the owner was Mr. W. S. Wall. Hops were grown in a yard next to the main road near Belmont.

Today the house retains its privacy but is surrounded by a huge housing estate and is now used as a home for the elderly called Barwood House, which has about half a mile of river bank for the use of its residents. The oast house was demolished some years ago.

Convent of Poor Clares, Bullingham Hereford. The Extern House.

In 1880 Mr Charles de la Barr Bodenham and his countess wife Irene donated land to the Sisters of the Order of St. Clare. The convent foundation stone was laid on September 8th 1885 and the nuns moved in on August 23rd 1886 to live a contemplative and industrious life. Over the years improvements and extensions were made, a cemetery blessed and a cottage built for the gardener and visiting priests. The nuns baked altar bread and packaged it as a source of income. The chapel is on the left of this photograph.

During the 1990's the nuns found that their quiet environment and privacy was being eroded by building developments so they decided to sell and move to a new building at Much Birch. Their old convent was demolished and the area developed into a housing estate by Westbury's (which sold the new homes at prices up to £100,000.)

The new convent stands on a hill site at Much Birch.

At the turn of the century there were two licensed premises which had the name Greyhound, the Greyhound Dog on the Belmont Road and the Greyhound Hotel at 88 Eign Street. This photograph was taken from the north end of Broad Street. The end wall of the hotel faces into All Saints Passage and the west end of the church. It was described as one of the best hotels in the city and had a medieval cellar.

By 1924 the ground floor had been converted into a drapers shop called Witts and Cole. Today a similar arrangement exists with a shop on the ground floor and the offices above have their entrance in All Saints Passage.

This photograph of the west end of Eign Street was taken in 1955. The closed shop was Astons, a furniture shop, which together with the neighbouring buildings, was soon to be demolished. The shop on the left was a butchers owned by Mrs. Norton, next was Max Shepherd a grocer and then a wallpaper shop next door. The pale building in the centre was Parry a butcher and the Red Lion Hotel is in the far distance. To the right is the Three Crowns Hotel sign.

The new buildings were set further back in order for the road to be widened.

In 1906 Hereford was the host city for The Three Choirs Festival. This is one of several decorative arches erected by the City Corporation near the junction with Edgar Street and Victoria Street. On the right is Arthur Edwards a hairdressers, whose hanging sign reads "Hair Cutting – Shampooing Rooms". The painted wall advertisement is for Clarksons who produced brooms, brushes, sponges, patent medicines etc. The union flags are flying from the Maidenhead Inn. In the far distance there is an advertisement for Deans Supply Stores, which sold cocoa, coffee and groceries.

This corner of the city could not have changed much more following the building of the inner relief road.

In the late 1930's the police used to purchase their cars from the County Motors and Motor Engineers at 57 Eign Street. This photograph taken in 1937 is of 4 new cars. There are two Morris cars on the left and the other two are Rovers. On the right stands Inspector Tom Wheeler, who later became Chief Constable. The shop behind the County School of Motoring sign was Madame Paula, a ladies hairdresser.

There is still a garage on this site which has expanded over the years. Today the business is Steels Westgate Ltd., who are the main dealers for Honda and Fiat.

Hereford had five turnpike gates around its centre and this photograph of the Whitecross Road gate was taken from the city side looking out of town. There are almshouses on the right and to the left is the toll house where tolls were extracted from passengers in vehicles to pay for the upkeep of the road. Most were established in 1663 and those in the city abolished in 1870. Later the local government Act of 1888 made road maintenance the responsibility of the local authority.

Today the toll house, gates and almshouses have gone. The house on the left has been named The Toll House and on the other side of the road is a modern development of almshouses.

At the junction of the Credenhill and Brecon roads is the Kings Acre Halt Garage. This 1948 photograph shows the early Edwardian garage with a late 1930's car at the petrol pumps. In 1934, the owner Mr. Hubert Powell advertised his business as a filling station, car park and convenience shop with accommodation, teas and refreshments for motorists. By 1948 he was also offering car servicing, over-hauls, re-boring, welding and vulcanising for cars, repairs and servicing for all makes of tractors too.

Today the business has been in the ownership of the Edmunds family for over 30 years. It is most interesting to note that the original garage building survives and is in full use, but this is only obvious to the visitor who looks up. The modern forecourt canopy which is very extensive hides the original building. Self service petrol pumps have replaced the old pumps which used to be operated by an attendant.

This postcard is marked Hereford Regatta 1907. The pleasure boat with the drapes has 4 women and a man on board and the coxed four in their boat are attended by an official on the floating pontoon. The Hereford Rowing Club was founded in 1860 and the first City Regatta which included a swimming gala was held in 1866. The terraced houses on the left are in Station Road and were built in 1896.

The new boat house was built in 1955 and then later in 1958 the old club house was demolished and rebuilt. Since the Rowing Club was founded there have been a total of 46 club captains.

For nearly 80 years there was a pleasure boat hire service on the Wye operated by Jordan's Boat Yard which was on the south bank of the river opposite the Greyfriars. The wooden steps lead down to the shore where several boats are moored. The tall stone building is all that was left of the Abergavenny and Hereford Tramway terminus and ticket office, which was opened on September 21st 1829. It closed on May 1st 1853 when the steam railway was built. This photograph was taken just before the buildings were demolished to make way for the new bridge.

The view today is not exciting but it is evident that the river bank has been protected against erosion.

This photograph of the Crown Inn in St. Martins' Street was taken at the turn of the century and shows a group of the regulars about to set off for an outing on their charabanc. The landlord was R. W. Hughes whose name appears on the pub sign.

In 1993 the building was extensively rebuilt and modernised and reopened with a new name – The Treacle Mine.

Was she or wasn't she born in Hereford? Nell Gwynne (1650-1687) is believed to have been born in Pipewell Street later re-named Gwynne Street, which was described as "a dingy, narrow ill paved thorough-fare" with the Bishops Palace garden wall on one side. Her grandson James Beauclerk became a Bishop of Hereford. The cottage where she is supposed to have been born was demolished in 1859 just after this early photograph was taken.

There is very little to identify the exact spot of Nell Gwynne's birthplace though there is a plaque, put up by the City Council, to mark the approximate site of the cottage. Only one building in the background survives.

The cart belonging to the Herefordshire Fruit Co., producers of Wye Valley Preserves stands outside their newly acquired building in West Street. The fruit business was started in 1886 by George Wright and carried on by his sons William and Sidney. This photograph was taken for their 1919 brochure in which they state that this building measured 53 feet by 36 feet with four storeys.

The street today has been largely rebuilt with an assortment of designs.

For nearly sixty years a large factory stood in the city centre and this photograph, taken in 1919, shows the entrance in Wall Street into the Wye Valley Preserves jam factory. On the ornamental arch is the foundation date of 1913. During their first year the factory had sales of £4,000 which by 1919 had risen to £217,000, quite an extraordinary rate of growth. The main office was in the Mansion House above Wright's farm produce shop in Widemarsh Street. The factory was large enough to make use of an overhead electric transporter from the stores behind the Mansion House to the jam building which was adjacent to the Imperial Brewery.

The site is now a landscaped car park which belongs to Tesco.

CORNER OF **BULMER'S** CASK FILLING ROOM
Hereford.

The early origins of cider making in the county are unknown but there are many references in literature including one in the 16th century Cider Bible now in the Mappa Mundi exhibition in Hereford Cathedral. Percy Bulmer began cider making at his parents home in 1887. Later in the following year production started in Ryeland Street where it remained for nearly a century. This postcard is of the cask filling room about 1920. Production was slow since it involved filling each wooden cask by hand.

Production of the wooden cask ceased many years ago and now casks are made of metal and are filled by a fully automated machine. A demonstration of wooden cask making can be seen at certain times in the nearby Cider Museum.

"Dégorgement" of Champagne Cider.
BULMER'S CELLARS, HEREFORD.

In 1892 Percy Bulmer decided to increase his knowledge of cider making so he went to Epernay, France. While there he learnt how to produce a champagne cider which was made in Hereford from 1906. This postcard view is of the machine which corked the bottles after removing the fermentation sediment. This was done by freezing the top two inches, drawing the first cork, the plug of ice then shot out, the contents were topped up, re-corked and foiled as seen in this picture. This process is known as disgorging.

Production of the Champagne Cider in Hereford ceased some years ago but continues in Belgium. However they still have to fill bottles and this photograph is of the latest machinery which can fill a vast number of bottles every hour. Today Bulmers is the largest producer of cider in this country. They are located on a new site at Moorfields but it is only a few hundred yards away from the original factory.

The photographer took this photograph looking along Bewell Street towards Widemarsh Street where the Temperance Hotel can be seen in the distance. There was a second hand clothes dealer in the end house of Bewell Street and a lodging house next door. The timber framed building has had many alterations done over the years. The 'For Sale' wall poster is advertising Mr. Mariott's auction on July 29th 1919 of a shop at 13 High Street and a dwelling house with three cottages in Bewell Street.

The half-timbered building and cottages have gone to make way for the large shop originally built by Marks & Spencer which was opened in 1920.

This early photograph shows a large area of Hereford from above the Moorfields area looking towards the Cathedral and River Wye. The large houses in the foreground are in Edgar Street and the Cattle Market is nearby. The road which crosses the photograph is Newmarket Street. The church is All Saints and the Bowling Green is just in front. The river meanders under the Victoria Bridge into the distance.

A recent helicopter flight reveals the new Hereford. In the foreground the corner of the Cattle Market is visible adjacent to the large roundabout with Tesco and its car park. Many other changes can be seen. *Photograph taken from an M. D. Air Services Helicopter.*

Hereford

This photograph of 1907 remained unidentified for many years but recently the author discovered that the houses are in Scudamore Street and was taken by the photographer standing in Clifford Street. The house on the left was called 'The Castle' and had two identical gates.

'The Castle' was demolished in 1970 and replaced by a semi-detached house.

Hereford had very few large houses in the city. This is Hampton Grange in Hampton Park Road about 1916 which stands high on the bank above the River Wye. It was built in 1898 for Mr Godwin who owned the tile works at Lugwardine. By the start of the first World War the house was owned by Councillor Edmund Robert Dymond who was made Mayor of Hereford on November 9th 1916. During the first World War the Red Cross Hereford Detachment under the command of Miss Ida Lea used the house as a hospital which started off with 25 beds in May 1915. The hospital was closed on February 28th 1919, by which time 873 patients had been treated here .

The house has been extended over the years to increase its accommodation as a nursing home for the blind. Its present use is as a nursing home for not only the blind but also for those with other disabilities.

Lower House Farm stands just outside the city on the old Ledbury Road near Tupsley Pitch close to Netherwood House. This photograph was taken in 1995 when the Herefordshire Nature Trust Ltd. purchased the house and the 42 acres of land around it. It was built around 1615 and over the years had little work done on it so that it was in a very poor state of repair and covered in stucco. The house has a view over the Lugg meadows towards Lugwardine.

Restoration of this building was carried out by a local firm, Dimbylow Crump and the total cost, together with the purchase price, was over £400,000, all of which was raised by the trust and included a generous donation from the Heritage Lottery Fund.

Westfields Street, Westfields.
HEREFORD

After the first World War Westfields was a small suburb with just a few houses in Highmore Street and Westfield Street. This view shows a rough road without raised pavements or gas lights. The motor car in the distance may be a visiting taxi. Some of the residents were listed as postman, gardener, jeweller, clerk, bricklayer, commercial traveller and journalist. On the left is Arkwright Terrace built in 1894. The house at the far end is in Clyde Street.

Over the years Westfields has become extensively developed and all gaps between the houses have been built on. Most residents now have cars which have to be parked in the road.

It was early this century that we began to understand about the spread of infection and the importance of isolation especially with diseases such as TB, diphtheria and smallpox so several isolation hospitals were built in and near Hereford. This photograph is of the isolation hospital at Credenhill, which was set back several hundred yards away from the Credenhill to Burghill road. It was built early this century soon after the purchase of land from the Guy's Hospital Estate in October 1903 – 3½ acres for £175. The windmill stands over a well and the low building on the left was used as changing rooms. The house may have been used as a cookhouse and provided accommodation for the staff. The main wards were in the next block while the building on the right was a laundry and mortuary.

In 1985 the premises were sold by the Health Authority to a private purchaser who extended and extensively refurbished the buildings and then opened them up as the Stretton Nursing Home with 52 beds. The home is in a beautiful, peaceful area.

This imposing building is Munstone House just north of the city in the parish of Holmer and Shelwick. This photograph taken around 1914 is of the owner Miss Burdon who travelled the world and brought back many exotic plants which survived for over half a century in her garden.

According to a recent sales brochure for the house there are 1½ acres of garden and the largest room is 29 feet by 16 feet and is used as a billiard room. The house is now a country house hotel and has had several extensions built on.

This looks like a factory in the open countryside, however it is an aerial view of Widemarsh Common and William Evans & Co., a large cider manufacturing company who were also pectin producers. The common and sports pavilion are visible. In the background is the Hay railway line with a locomotive and goods trucks. The large building behind the factory is called Moor House and was owned by the Chave family of Chave and Jackson Chemists. Canon Moor Farm can just be seen on the horizon.

Today the view has changed considerably and only the site of the railway track remains and Moor House can just be seen below the smoke in the field. The old factory has been demolished and a block of flats with a central arch erected. The vast roof, which was destroyed recently by a large fire, belongs to Sun Valley Poultry *This photograph was taken from a M. D. Air Services helicopter.*

The old stone Wye Bridge was the only passenger and vehicle river crossing for many miles both up and down stream. With the approach of Queen Victoria's Diamond Jubilee several suggestions were put forward to the Corporation and general public as how to celebrate this event. A footbridge was chosen, which was to be erected near the Castle Green and General Hospital. Money was raised by public subscription, and constructed entirely by Corporation workers at a cost of £1,200. The bridge replaced a ferry. The ferry hut, winding point, machinery and slip-way are visible. The small ferry boat in the middle of the river has one passenger.

This is a photograph taken in the rain of the opening ceremony.

The bridge was designed by city surveyor Mr John Parker. The piers and abutments were made of concrete. A city store owner and councillor, Mr Augustus Edwards, was involved with the bridge from inception to completion. It was formerly opened by Lady Emily Foley on September 29th 1898.

List of Places